Dreams & Memories

Paintings and Stories
by Joan T. Sherman

Love in a Cornfield, January 15, 1992

Published by

Acknowledgements

Editor: Jean Hurley
Secretary: Margo Ellis
Photographer: Perry Conley
Design and Production: Sheri Connell

Copyright © 1993 by Joan T. Sherman
All rights reserved. No part of this publication may be reproduced without prior permission of the publisher.

Published by

Heart's Desire
P.O. Box 187
Madison, NH 03849-0187

First Edition

Library of Congress Catalog Card Number: 94-96355

ISBN 0-9642424-0

Printed in the United States of America

*Dedicated to Paul D. Lidstrom, M.D.,
who gave me the encouragement to be
audacious enough to paint and write.*

Table of Contents

	Page
Foreword	7
Artist's Statement	9
The Crab Thing	13
Music to the People	17
Territories, Great Neck, 1938	19
Annapolis, 1949	23
Phipps Clinic	27
Love in a Cornfield	31
Garden of Eden	35
Death of My Mother	37
Halloween	39
Just Above Water	43
War and Peace	45
Facing Mecca	47
Two-Minute Poses	51
Family Tree, 1992	53
The Holy Spirit	57
Afterword	59
About the Artist	63

FOREWORD

Many people think that being oneself is one of the easiest things in the world. Not so. The struggle to be an individual is a difficult one. At any given time there are many forces at work within and without that serve to distract us from hearing the still small voice that would direct our being in the world. And, as Alice Miller and others have shown, an excessive demand for socialization in childhood often dims even the brightest human spirit early on, setting the stage for depression later in life.

Depression steals upon the soul like nightfall. The current vogue is to understand it as a biological process reflecting disruptions in neurotransmitter systems, and yet it is also something more. Depression is a great inner disquietude, a debilitating condition in which one's energies no longer connect meaningfully with the world. Born of frustration, depression is a heavy darkness that cannot be willed away; it forces one's eyes to turn inward. Under the best of circumstances, depression is a dark night which can lead to a dawn of new understanding, and to a kind of rebirth. And this ultimately is the goal of psychotherapy.

The deep and persistent sadness that led Joan Sherman into psychotherapy is the same sadness that led her toward self-discovery and to new creative life. The strikingly vivid, sometimes haunting, and always expressive paintings reproduced in this book emerged spontaneously during the course of her treatment, in the form of dreams and memories, as the title of her book suggests. They represent her efforts to re-member her life and to integrate the various forces at work within it. The reader who has eyes to see will note the gradual transformation of various images having to do with her inner world, from the darkness of the opening, where the "crab thing" has gotten hold of her at night, to the rising of the sun in the *Garden of Eden*, where all things are made new. One can see that the images from the unconscious become less threatening as they are worked with. Initially crab-like and dangerous, the water denizens become almost companionable by the time of *Just Above Water*. And her deepening reorientation toward life is apparent in *Facing Mecca*, where, turning to the East, the direction of dawn, the author finds that contemplative solitude which is, to use her words, "Home at last." Home rests atop the integrative mandala on the Persian rug, a *paradeisos* where opposing forces meet, bringing respite and contentment. Psychologically this corresponds to the discovery of that quiet center within the soul where speaks the still small voice. The answer to despair is found here, in an attitude of obeisance to a higher order found within.

The images within this book touch on universal themes, and so I recommend it to all who are interested in the inner workings of the soul, to those who are interested in art, and to all those who are interested in the art of living.

Paul D. Lidstrom, M.D.
January 10, 1994

ARTIST'S STATEMENT

In 1949, while recovering from a nervous breakdown, I painted my first picture, *Annapolis, 1949*. I was nineteen, and even then had it in my mind to paint more pictures in this style.

Many years were spent raising a family and managing a small radio station with my husband. During those years I worked in crafts, particularly fiber arts. The League of New Hampshire Craftsmen, Conways' Home Industries and the Southern Maine Chapter of the Embroiderers' Guild provided classes and workshops for an eager student. The Mount Washington Valley Arts Association and the School for Lifelong Learning introduced me to classes in fine art, including drawing and watercolor painting.

I spent the winter of 1991 as a degree student at the Savannah College of Art and Design (SCAD), studying drawing, paper making and basketry. During the 1991-92 academic year, I took drawing and painting at the Portland School of Art.

I have been influenced by American folk and primitive art, traditional rug hooking, and the arts and crafts, people and landscapes, and music and color of Mexico. I have visited Mexico nine times. In 1991, at SCAD, I discovered Frida Kahlo - both her paintings and her life story. In January, 1992, I saw the show "Images of the Bleeding Heart," an exhibit of contemporary Mexican artists at the Museum of Contemporary Art in Boston. This show moved me deeply.

I started painting these pictures in July, 1991, as a continuation of what I had started with *Annapolis, 1949*. **Dreams & Memories** are just that: illustrations of my dreams and memories.

Dreams & Memories was first presented at the Idia Center, in Intervale, New Hampshire, from August 18 to September 14, 1992. I am most grateful to Dia Stolnitz, the Director of the Idia Center for spurring me on to "get it all together," and for giving me the opportunity to show my work to the public. I have added five new paintings since September, 1992: *Halloween, The Holy Spirit, Just Above Water, War and Peace*, and *Facing Mecca*. David C. Baker has been very helpful in critiquing my efforts since January, 1993.

I felt that the loving, encouraging atmosphere of The Jumping Off Place, a spiritual book shop, would be ideal for showing *Dreams & Memories*, with the addition of the five new paintings. Ginger Blymer, its founder, enthusiastically agreed. As she is most interested in dreams and their interpretation, she has many books about dreams available.

Dreams & Memories is an expression of my lifelong search for mental health and artistic expression. This show is dedicated to Paul D. Lidstrom, who gave me encouragement to be audacious enough to paint and write.

         Joan T. Sherman
         May 31, 1993

The Crab Thing, August 10, 1991

THE CRAB THING

Her family lived on Long Island by the Sound, when she was three. She played happily in the sand by the water's edge in the warm sun. The world was a good and wonderful place and there was no evil.

One day a medium-sized boy came screaming out of the water with a large crab firmly attached to one of his big toes. He was terrified. His mother had a hard time detaching the crab from the boy's toe and an even harder time calming his terror.

The boy's terror was instantly transmitted to the little girl. Yes, there was evil and danger in the world, hidden and unseen, ready to attack when least expected, beneath the calm waters of the Sound.

That night, a nightmare came to her. The crab thing was in her bed, biting her big toe. Neither mother nor father could convince her it wasn't true. To the despair of her parents, the nightmare came back night after night.

For the next sixty years, the crab thing menaced her dreams. In this dream she is a woman, gone for a skinny dip in the secluded pond in New Hampshire where her parents had built a summer cottage. The beavers had been at work flooding the woods and had killed the trees. Summer is over and the summer people have gone back to their cities. It is dusk. The moon is out. The evening star Mars, God of War, has risen. She swims far into the mirror-like pond still warm from hot summer days just past. She comes to the white rowboat that had belonged to her father. Being tired from her swim, she clambers into the rowboat. As it begins to sink, she understands that the rowboat is the symbol of death and not of safety as she had supposed.

The crab thing attacks, springing suddenly from the water. She fights the crab thing tooth and nail, finally defeating him, only to be menaced by a shark and the snapping turtle that lurks in the weeds on the bottom of the murky pond. She remembers Perley Ward, the hired man, who had warned her not to swim in the pond. Perley said there were dangerous killer snapping turtles, and that sharks had swum from the ocean up the rivers, streams and brooks into the pond. She had laughed at Perley, but the shark and snapping turtle were real enough in her dream.

In life, her father had been a lawyer and his ashes were in the pond that he had loved. He appears as Poseidon, god of watery depths with its hidden terrors. He holds the trident in one hand, symbol of his power, and the balancing scales of Justice in the other. He does nothing to help her and stares impassively ahead as he lets be what will be. Her mother appears as an angel, powerless to help her, praying for her safety.

Music to the People, September 25, 1991

MUSIC TO THE PEOPLE

She dreamed that she was a little girl again, longing to study music and grow up to be an opera star. Her family was not musical and her dream of even attending an operatic performance was out of the question. She listened to the opera on the radio and let the waves of emotion flow through her.

In her dream, the Diva of the Metropolitan Opera Company comes to her neighborhood in the musicmobile on a Sunday afternoon to sing for the people. The Diva wears a shimmering white chiffon gown, sparkling with golden beads. Her hair is golden too, and she has a golden soprano voice. Not an eye is dry as the Diva sings of the love of Mimi and Rudolfo.

The people in the neighborhood open their doors and hearts to the music of the Diva. The young Italian leans from the balcony in his pink villa already in love with the Diva. Junior and his mother come out to see, hear, and feel the music. Handsome Jim and his dog, Rebel, bask in the Diva's aria, while Jim's little sister, Ann, watches from an upstairs window.

As a little girl, she had longed to sing like the Diva and have a handsome Italian admirer. She had wished she could play with the children across the street but she was shy and afraid the other children wouldn't like her. The sidewalk was a barrier not only to becoming friends with the other children, but to her dream of studying music and the opera.

She holds a red balloon which is a symbol of her heart - an offering to the Diva and to the children across the street.

The stalwart and faithful Bluebird guards her happiness and her pussycat is her only true friend and playmate.

Territories, Great Neck, 1938, January 31, 1992

TERRITORIES, GREAT NECK, 1938

Mr. Brown, Mr. Watson and Mr. T. were neighbors in Great Neck, a suburb of New York City, during the Great Depression of the 1930's. All three of them guarded their property - their small rectangles of green earth, houses and gardens, garages and cars. They fenced off their "territories" with different kinds of fences: white picket fences, garden gates, gentle evergreens, and even barbed wire! The three men barely spoke, even though Mr. Watson and Mr. T. both had gone to Yale. Their wives did not become close friends either, but their children crossed the barriers of the territories.

Mr. Watson had the toughest time of the three men, trying to get ahead in the coal business. Mr. T. had a good position as a junior partner in a large Wall Street law firm, and was better off than Mr. Watson. But Mr. Brown - he was actually prosperous! He owned a seed and garden business, and it was flourishing. Mr. Brown was doing so well he could afford to buy the vacant lot behind his house, which he turned into a big garden complete with a goldfish pond, a weeping willow, and a waterfall. The tree in his front yard was an exotic oriental, his soil was richer and darker, and his lawn was greener. He had two brand new Buicks, and an overhead garage door, the first of its kind seen anywhere. Mr. Brown bought his son, Bo, a real gasoline-powered, gold car. Bo drove it all over the neighborhood. The children weren't allowed to play in Mr. Brown's territory, only on the surrounding sidewalks, streets and vacant lots.

Mr. and Mrs. T. had no gardening skills and could barely grow grass. Their yard was mostly dandelions, and the dead blossoms, blown by the wind, seeded Mr. Brown's immaculate lawn. Carl, Mr. Brown's hired German gardener, patiently, on his knees, cut the weeds and dandelions out of Mr. Brown's lawn with a forked hand tool. But the T.'s were neat, and Mr. T. carefully raked the leaves from under his maple tree, and more carefully burned the leaves, while his dog, Chips, and the family cat, Black Roseberry, watched. Mr. T. had already washed his new blue Ford V8 (his pride and joy), just the right car for a junior partner at Satterlee and Canfield.

Mr. T. had built a roomy sandbox for his two little girls, Joan and Gretchen. The sisters spent many happy hours together building sand castles in that sandbox. Junior Watson, Mr. Watson's older son, had first seen the pretty little girls playing in the sandbox just after the T.'s had moved to Great Neck. Junior crossed the barbed wire fence to get to know them.

The big feature of the Watson's yard was an enormous apple tree. Mr. Watson had constructed a two-story tree house in it. It had ladders and a garden hose attached to the lower story that served as an escape, like the pole for the firemen at the fire house, just up the hill. Junior was given a second-hand bicycle, all they could afford in hard times. His faithful black Scottie, Booty, went wherever he went. Mr. Watson had to depend on an old black Packard to take him on his rounds selling coal, and like an old shoe, it was very comfortable.

Junior was the oldest, then Joan, and then Bo. Junior and Bo were wary of each other, both being boys. Junior and Joan agreed that Bo was a sissy. Joan played with both of them, first one and then the other, unconsciously making them jealous. Junior could be bossy and superior - a male chauvinist. When

Junior was just "too much," Joan played with Bo, when she, being older, could be the bossy one.

Junior resented the Brown's affluence, and particularly hated the Brown's back garden that had once been the vacant lot where all the kids played softball. Bo didn't let any of the kids ride in his gas-powered car, either. Another sore point!

In the fall, Junior got even by throwing apples into Mr. Brown's fish pond from the upper story of the tree house, as Joan watched with glee. The sun was going down and the lights were coming on in the buildings on the skyline of New York, that could be seen from the top story of the tree house. Soon Junior, Joan and Bo would be called in to supper. They each would pop popcorn in their livingroom fireplaces while listening to Jack Benny on the radio.

What ever happened to the "gas man" and those peaceful Sundays in the suburbs?

Annapolis, 1949, April 30, 1949

ANNAPOLIS, 1949

They had lived in this room in Annapolis while she went to music school and her husband was in college. She was a young bride of nineteen, expecting her first child. Pregnancy played a cruel trick and she had a nervous breakdown.

While recovering in a mental hospital, The Institute of Living, in Hartford, Connecticut, she longed to be back in Annapolis with her husband. She found some oil paints in the occupational therapy room and painted this nostalgic picture of their room in Annapolis that had been a place of such happiness.

A college classmate, Gene Thaw, gave the couple an old commode, and her husband bought components to turn it into a hi-fi cabinet. The couple lovingly refinished it and it was a central part of their lives, as she was a music student and he a jazz buff. He made a bookshelf, with great difficulty, and finally kept it from collapsing by bracing it diagonally with boards nailed to the back. Patrick Davis, another classmate, taught her to make braided rugs out of old clothes. They were proud of their accomplishments. They played tennis and walked in the rain. The fireplace worked and that winter they found wood for it and gave parties in front of the fire. Spaghetti was their great culinary achievement, served with Chianti, a green salad and garlic bread.

In the mornings, they ground Mocha Java coffee beans, bought in the market in Baltimore, in an antique, hand-turned coffee grinder he had given her as an engagement present. The smell of their coffee filled the boarding house.

Miniature paintings of her father's ancestors and an old bottle filled with bittersweet she had picked in the fall, reminded her of her mother and father and the childhood home she had so recently left.

It took her nearly three months to patiently paint this picture. When it was finished, they let her go home to bring a lovely little girl into the world.

She vowed that someday she would paint more pictures of her **Dreams & Memories**.

Phipps Clinic, November 7, 1991

PHIPPS CLINIC

Suddenly she was sick - very sick - mentally ill. It was an emergency! Sick as she was, she knew she must go to the hospital. She was a bride of eight months, almost five months pregnant and only nineteen. It was January in Baltimore, cold and bleak, with freezing rain. Her young husband took her to Phipps Clinic, a reputable hospital for the mentally ill. Here, she believed, she would find peace and quiet in a private room, an understanding doctor to listen to her and to care. Perhaps she might even learn handweaving in occupational therapy.

This was not the case. She was taken to a gray, locked and barred ward, where women were screaming. She was stripped of all her clothing and possessions, including her wedding ring, glasses and toothbrush. This was the accepted, approved method of treating the mentally ill. It was bedlam: the "snake pit" of the 1940's.

Unspeakable things were done to her - life-threatening things in the name of "treatment." Dr. Kelly and Big Nurse were good Christian folk who believed in their cure and thought it was a kindness, but their belief only increased her anger and confusion. How could they not know their "treatment" was dangerous as well as cruel? Dr. Kelly, she learned, was planning a legal, therapeutic abortion even though she was five months pregnant, if she did not quickly repond to his "treatment." He believed that his unholy regimen of barbituates, peraldehyde, degradation, deprivation, physical restraints, force and confinement would bring her health, happiness and sanity. Terrified, she told herself that she must pretend to be normal and sane, no matter how difficult, in order to save herself and her child. In this she succeeded. Dr. Kelly thought she was really getting better. He was unaware that she was fooling him. He spared her child.

She had been in Phipps Clinic a month before her husband, father and father-in-law could arrange a transfer to a gentler, kinder hospital in Hartford. She left Phipp's Clinic exhausted, still terribly sick, even more mentally disturbed, and weighing less than ninety pounds. The experience left her with recurring nightmares. Waves of hatred would wash over her not only in dreams, but in waking moments too, so severe as to be immobilizing. The experience had been a near fatal trauma and there was no way to process it, until psychotherapy rescued her from the grip of its memory when she was in her early sixties.

In this dream, forty-four years later, she relives the moment she had learned of Dr. Kelly's plan to abort her child. She is naked in the gray, barren, locked and barred ward. Somehow the Bluebird of Happiness is there to protect her, but the Crab Thing, now with the wings of a hornet, flies in to defeat the Bluebird, once and for all. She, who had been a voice student, sings of her horror and fury and her love for the mortally wounded Bluebird. She knows her singing will unnerve her jailers. Her unborn child, a winged cherub, smiles blissfully in her womb, unaware of the mayhem and danger in Phipps Clinic.

Love in a Cornfield, January 15, 1992

LOVE IN A CORNFIELD

The young man from the East brings his wife back to his ancestors' farm in Illinois, just in time for Sunday dinner. The platters are piled high with fried chicken, mashed potatoes, pan gravy, Kentucky Wonders, and summer squash. There is homemade corn relish, bread and butter pickles, farm-churned butter and strawberry jam to spread on home-baked, whole wheat bread. For dessert, there are fresh peaches from the peach orchard and Industrial Union cake, a specialty of the farm.

The conversation at dinner is about the futures market in corn, soy beans and hog bellies. What will Washington's position be next year on subsidies? When is the best time to tell the tenant farmers to harvest and sell the corn and soy beans, the hogs and the cattle? Which of the Black Angus and Poland China hogs should go to the Illinois State Fair? The advantages and disadvantages of hybrid corn are discussed. Yes, the new corn is just right for the mechanical corn picker to harvest. It is pest resistant, but the kernels are so hard the hogs can hardly eat it, and the corn needs to be converted to bacon.

As a New York City girl, she is fascinated by this storybook, midwestern farm, so old and full of tradition. The deeds on the land were made out by Abraham Lincoln, when he rode circuit as a young lawyer. The story has it that a reprobate cousin cut Lincoln's signatures off the deeds and sold them for hard liquor. Before there was a big New England-style farm house, built with the black walnut trees that grew on the hill, the family lived in a log cabin. At night the wolves had prowled about the cabin, their red eyes glaring through the chinks of the walls. Three kiln-loads of brick were rejected as not good enough for the homestead before the patriarch decided to build with black walnut. Even the floors, now worn, were made of walnut.

The young man and his wife slept deeply in a big, black walnut bed. Breakfast was fresh farm eggs, yeast-risen buckwheat cakes and home-cured bacon from the cellar, a cellar kept cool by thick granite walls.

It's Monday, Mrs. Kipp has hung out the wash, fed the chickens and canned yellow freestone peaches, and left them to cool on the zinc table in the screened summer kitchen. Peach cobbler and left-over fried chicken, wrapped in starched linen napkins, on blue china plates, have been put in the pie safe for the noonday meal.

The young man takes his wife for a tour of the farm. The hot sun seems to pull the corn and soy beans out of the ground toward the sky. The dew has just dried from the grass. The doves coo in the hay loft and the cat, Oscar, guardian of the hearth, suns himself in the yard. The newly freshened Black Angus cow suckles her calf. Two Poland China hogs root for nuts in the black walnut grove on the hill. Barn swallows swoop and cry as they pick bugs out of the air. The soy beans ripple in the distance, in the field on the back forty.

The young man takes his wife into a corn field. He makes love to her on the warm, deep, rich, forgiving, Illinois earth, hidden by the dancing, ripening corn. The cricket sings his rasping love song to them, while his ancestors watch from the family graveyard. The ancestors hope that the young man and his wife will bring new and continuing life to this ancient land. The Bluebird of Happiness watches with great satisfaction from a branch of a black walnut tree.

All this the young wife, now grown old, remembers as she looks at the Tiffany, mine-cut, diamond ring she wears, that had belonged to old Auntie; that old Auntie left to Aunt Louise; that Aunt Louise left to Gwendolyn; that Gwendolyn gave to the young man, who gave it to the young woman when they had become engaged.

Garden of Eden, July 15, 1991

THE GARDEN OF EDEN

She dreamed she was Eve in the Garden of Eden: the embodiment of all women, the connection between the center of the earth and the heavens.

It is spring and the heat from the center of earth warms the waters beneath the earth and sends it, like quicksilver, through the bedrock, topsoil and vegetation through the center of her being. The quicksilver boils through the top of her head to the cloud, who is Adam. Adam receives the power of the center of the earth as transmitted through the essential woman. He drinks her strength, only to transform the quicksilver into gentle rain to water the earth, to bring forth life and replenish the waters beneath the earth.

Eve stands solidly in the bedrock, the strong, firm bone of the earth where diamonds are made, indicating her value. The Tree of Life bares the pierced heart of the love Adam and Eve have for each other. The Bluebird of Happiness stands on a branch of the tree, watching and confirming God's plan for love and procreation, in spite of God's charge that Adam and Eve remain children and celibate.

The sun is rising in the heavens to bring warmth and life to the earth from above. The water and heat nurture waterlilies and cattails, trees and flowers; the mountains sing a celebration of life. The fish in the pond are spawning and the Frog Prince is waiting to be kissed. The Grandfather and Grandmother of all life, now diminished in old age, appear as daddy-long-legs and his lady bug.

The snake reminds us of the deception, evil, suffering and death of all life on earth.

Death of My Mother, February 29, 1992

DEATH OF MY MOTHER

Alice took many years to die of Alzheimer's disease. She was in the nursing home for the last five years of her life. She loved it there, where everyone treated her like a little princess.

They called one Tuesday and said she had taken a turn for the worse, and that it wouldn't be long. The family gathered and we took turns sitting with her, talking to her, caressing her and holding her hand.

I was sitting with her one night a week later, during our vigil, and dozed off. I dreamed that she has just died, her happy spirit, free at last, ascending into Heaven. In my dream, she returns to greet me through the door of her room in the nursing home. She is young and beautiful, healthy and glamorous. I hold her hand as her beloved little girl.

I awoke with a start to find Mr. Pickwick, the nursing home cat, snuggled against her. Mr. Pickwick was a black cat, who had greeted my mother on her arrival at the nursing home five years before. Alice loved cats, particularly Mr. Pickwick. He had a "cat ministry" in the nursing home that was uncanny.

Alice had indeed quietly crossed the River Styx, with Mr. Pickwick by her side to ease her passage.

Halloween, November 15, 1992

HALLOWEEN

In October, 1992, I flew from Portland, Maine, to Portland, Oregon, to visit my kid brother and his family. My brother's family is an uproarious, rollicking handful, as four boys were born in five years. They are old enough now to be my special playmates, and they call me "Auntie Joanie."

I told the boys "Johnny and Martin" stories - the stories my Grandfather told my Father and my Father told to me. They listened with rapt attention and were soon making up their own "Johnny and Martin" stories to tell me.

Each day I entertained one of my nephews, one on one, at the Hotel Malory, in downtown Portland, where I was staying. We drew pictures, worked on embroidery, and each boy told me about his troubles and triumphs, at school and at home. We roamed the city, pretending to be the liberators of an oppressed Near Eastern nation. The afternoon ended with an elegant tea, brought to my suite by room service. We savored the tea in our tent made of blankets thrown over chairs and planned a glorious democracy for our liberated country.

One night, I told the boys that if they rubbed my "vanishing cream" on their faces, they would simply vanish and be invisible to all but each other. I explained that it only worked on little boys and that on old ladies, like me, the vanishing cream was supposed to make my wrinkles vanish. They looked dubious about my wrinkles, but were delighted to rub the cream on their faces and disappear. We played this make-believe until bedtime, when I explained that the vanishing cream only worked for a few hours, before its magic wore off.

We also played games, took walks, and worked on craft projects. We rode MAX, the interurban, to the Saturday Market, ate at MacDonald's and watched Teenage Mutant Ninja Turtle videos. I visited their schools and told a "Johnny and Martin" story to Billy's preschool class. We watched Spencer kick a winning goal in his soccer league.

The big event, and the culmination of my visit, was Halloween. We had spent the afternoon making Prayer Arrows, the magical arrows of the Kuchema Indians, which I had learned to make in Mexico. The arrows were made of sticks my sister-in-law cut from a forsythia bush in her garden. A secret wish was then wrapped around the top of each arrow and colored yarn and metallic threads were wrapped around the whole stick, holding the message in place and making the arrow bright and colorful. Feathers were tied to the top of the arrows to help the arrows fly to the the Great Spirit. Roses from their mother's rose garden and mineral samples from the earth were tied to each arrow, as a final symbolic touch.

Michael, the youngest, wished for a Ninja Turtle costume to wear to the school Halloween party and for trick or treating that night. Billy, the next youngest, wished that he could have a fast red sports car when he grew up. Spencer, the next to oldest wished that everyone would be safe, and Eddie, the oldest, wished that there would be no more wars and that no one would ever go hungry again.

I had carefuly brought my Halloween costume with me. The big, black, Victorian velvet hat, with the Bluebird of Happiness pinned on it, arrived uncrushed from the East Coast. I dressed as Endora, the beautiful, sophisticated, good (if confused) Grandmother Witch, of the television series,

"Bewitched." Michael got his wish and wore his Ninja Turtle costume; Spencer was a ghost; Billy was Mickey Mouse and discovered that a tail is something everyone steps on; and Eddie was an Indian chief.

April, the faithful black Labrador, admired us all in our finery.

The Virgin Mary and the Christ Child watched over me and my joyous, loving and happy family from the painting over the sofa.

Just Above Water, January 31, 1993

JUST ABOVE WATER

Thanksgiving 1992 came and went. Life was peaceful, uneventful. The autumn colors had been particularly beautiful that year, in spite of dire predictions that pollution had so damaged the trees as to cause the fall colors to fade permanently, as they had faded the past two years. Our favorite time of the year is when the leaves are off the trees and the shape of the mountains can be seen. The fall air calls for long walks.

On November 30 we were called back to work. We held our noses and began. It was like cleaning the Augean stables! One day at a time, one foot in front of the other, lift one stone every day and you will build a New England stone wall. By the end of January, cold and bleak, with no snow in sight, I painted this picture of how I felt: *Just Above Water*. Here I sit, about to drown. The curious fish stare at me. I am an alien invading their territory. My hair, like seaweed, is blown by a relentless wind. The sun scorches me.

I remember,

> The Lord himself is thy keeper, the Lord
> is thy defense upon thy right hand;
> So that the sun shall not burn thee by day,
> neither the moon by night....
> The Lord shall preserve thy going out, and
> thy coming in, from this time forth, for evermore.
>
> Levalvi Oculos, Psalm CXXI

My painting amused me and restored my sense of humor.

War and Peace, March 31, 1993

WAR AND PEACE

By the first of March, the crisis at work was over. We could see the light at the end of the tunnel. The snow that came so late in the winter, brought business to our valley, and everyone was cheered by this benefit. Even though there would be still much to do, my husband and I felt we could take a short vacation to Florida.

Once in Florida, we both felt our complete exhaustion. He got sick immediately, running a fever for five days, and was forced to stay in bed. I lay awake at night, listening to him breathe, afraid he would stop. Like most sick men, he was cranky, angry, demanding and critical. I waited on him, hardly daring to leave him. I picked up my paints, to occupy my time and for the soothing therapy of painting my feelings.

I painted *War and Peace* about the ups and downs of married life. He is angry, withdrawn, and uncommunicative. I am just as angry, to the point of never wanting to see him again! Notice that we are, none-the-less, joined at the hip. This cold war too will pass, and we will be in a time of marital peace.

We lie on a blanket with a pattern of jungle flowers, as mankind is not far from its beginnings in the wild. The sea birds go on about their business, ignoring this couple and their struggle for serenity.

Facing Mecca, April 15, 1993

FACING MECCA

Home at last! But not until a hair-raising trip through the blizzard. Snow everywhere - beautiful to behold, but impossible to negotiate. My husband was still very sick, with coughing, congestion, fatigue and weakness, and still just as cranky. My own state was even more stressed than before our trip to Florida.

I started to go to AA meetings. I was surprised. The old timers I had known in the past and alcoholics' wives in ALANON, all practiced "tough love." My misconception that AA was an exercise in scolding and punishing those afflicted with alcoholism had prevented me from going in the past. It seemed to me that I had had enough of "tough love." The kindness, gentle love and caring I found in the halls of AA was overwhelming and contagious and not at all what I had feared.

As Nora did in *The Doll's House*, I had to escape from marriage and work.

> "Does it occur to you that this is the first
> time we two, you and I, husband and wife,
> have had a serious conversation?"
> "I must stand quite alone, if I am to under-
> stand myself and everything about me.
> It is for that reason that I cannot remain
> with you any longer."

I needed my own space, for the solitude, prayer and contemplation I had dreamed about for so long. The perfect place would be the cottage that my Father had built in the wilderness, on the pond with a view of the sun setting behind Mt. Chocorua. Finally unafraid that Old Crow would insidiously sneak up on me to rob me of the peace, joy and pleasure of such a retreat, I left home. I didn't fear my own company, or loneliness either.

I took my paints, my AA books, and toothbrush, and started my journey into sobriety. My AA friends and sponsor cheered me on. Family and friends supported me. At last I was free to turn off the TV set to watch the sunset, visit and talk with my friends and cook them supper. The courage came to me to tell the truth to my husband about my real feelings which had been hidden so long, not only from him, but from myself.

Facing Mecca is the picture of my retreat. It is noon; the sky is cloudless and bright; the pond is calm; branches in front of the window rustle in the light, warm, spring air. Mt. Chocorua and the Three Sisters, in their holiness, watch powerful and majestic, connecting the sky to the earth and water. Birds twitter and the peepers sing the song of the rebirth of life after the winter. Naked before God, I face East toward Mecca, kneeling on a prayer rug woven with flowers. The rug represents Paradise. The amaryllis that is supposed to bloom at Christmas decided to bloom in April. Its beauty is a sign that I will recover. The plate on the wall depicts the moon with Diana shooting for the stars. It is the symbol of the aspirations, strength, solidarity and mystique of women: mothers, sisters, daughters and lovers all.

Three weeks passed; I was restored, renewed and ready to go home to my husband, who was so patiently waiting for me.

Two-Minute Poses, May 26, 1992

TWO-MINUTE POSES

This is a self-portrait of the artist in her studio. The portrait reflects her memories of some sad and happy times in her past. Her sketches, drawn from life, hang on the wall behind her.

Family Tree, August 14, 1992

FAMILY TREE, 1992

Forty-three years of marriage have brought them through thick and thin to retirement. They live in an old gray farm house in the country, surrounded by fields, woods and mountains. The Tree of Life grows in their front yard. The Bluebird of Happiness, only found at home in your heart, has finally found a mate and is raising a family in the tree. The tree is strong and sends out leaves, for the descendants of this marriage.

The couple appear as they were when they were courting: he in a gray seersucker suit and she in a yellow dress, the height of fashion, the "New Look" of the late 1940's. In the heart carved on the tree so long ago, a radiant flower blooms. He holds a book, and his jazz records, tennis racket and ball are beside him as reminders of the interests of a lifetime. She holds her embroidery, and her paint palette is at her feet, indicating her serious pursuits. Marilyn Monroe, the gorgeous white and orange cat she had given him as a kitten for Christmas nine years ago, stands between them, pampered and adored. Oscar Wildecat was found starving, abandoned and terrified in the cellar, one freezing January day. He lives with them too, after being tamed and cared for through many illnesses.

The picture wouldn't be complete without the old, green truck that limps along hauling firewood, manure for the garden and garbage to the dump. Her gardens bloom with hollyhocks, old roses and zinnias - the old-fashioned flowers, for an old-fashioned family. The satellite dish and TV antenna on top of the house bring them in touch with the present. There is TV, music, laughter and tears in this house, and new life.

The sun beams down on this corner of God's creation, as it does on all the earth. "The family is greater than love itself."

The Holy Spirit, December 13, 1992

THE HOLY SPIRIT

My feet are firmly planted on the yellow ochre floor. Yellow ochre - the color is thick, torpid, viscous, cementing my feet to a life rooted in despair. My therapist, unafraid to get down on the yellow ochre floor, appears as my beloved black cat, Black Roseberry. Black Roseberry listened to me when I was a child, as my therapist patiently listens to me now. I sit on a green couch, as green is the color of healing. The paisley pattern on the couch resembles the tears I shed, unashamedly, but with great difficulty.

My naked body is symbolic of the naked truths I tell, and my hand rests over my aching heart.

The red plant is my violent emotions escaping, at last, from the prison of the blue vase of sadness. Even the wallpaper is blue with sadness, charged with a pattern of electric waves.

But the window is open to a rosy future, a sunny field and the delicious green of early spring. When I leave this place of love and healing, the Bluebird of Happiness, who has been protecting me, will fly over me as I drive through the magic mountains of New Hampshire toward the setting sun and home.

The Bluebird will make sure the lessons learned on the other side of the mountains are put into practice at home. Now I watch the Bluebird, "My Holy Spirit," flutter about my yard, find a mate, build a nest, raise a family, eat bugs and preen himself. He seems satisfied with a job well done. The Bluebird is only found in one's own backyard, but he will travel a great distance, over mountains and rivers, in winter and summer, to find help for the ones he loves.

AFTERWORD

A sadness had plagued me most of my life; a sadness so deep and so painful as to paralyze me, making the simplest task a monumental undertaking. I tried to find help when the sadness became unbearable, but professional help was either unavailable or inadequate, until very recently. The treatment of depressive illnesses has advanced to levels not dreamed of even a decade ago, and now it is widely available, even in rural America. Family physicians are aware of the disease. The public is being educated that depression is a real sickness that can be treated successfully, and that the mentally ill should not be regarded as "bad" or "undesirable." *The Holy Spirit* is a painting of my successful journey from the darkness of depression, to light, hope, and life.

I think my search for "the kind doctor, who would listen and care and encourage me to express myself," was the doctor I had expected to find at Phipps Clinic when I was nineteen. I am amazed at my persistence, born of desperation, and lasting more than forty years. Here is a brief history of my Odyssey.

My introduction to mental health care in 1949 was the Auschwitz punishment of Phipps Clinic. Next was the benign neglect at the Institute of Living, where, left to my own devices, I discovered the healing powers of painting and writing. A postpartum psychosis after the birth of our second child sent me to Craig House, where I experienced twenty-one massive, frightening, physically and mentally painful electric shock treatments, which, however painful, brought me out of psychosis to sanity and restored me to my family. No psychotherapy was offered to me at the Phipps Clinic, the Institute of Living or at Craig House.

Dr. Samuel B. Burchill, a powerful Park Avenue psychiatrist who had advised me and my family since the beginning of my illness, knew that another pregnancy could result in another psychotic episode, which could prove to be a permanent state for me. He wisely and kindly made sure this danger was past. I shudder to think of a life shut away in mental darkness in the locked back wards of the mental hospitals of that day - a life separated from my husband and children.

The ongoing symptoms of depression caused me to look for that "kind doctor" to talk to. My search took me to The Allan Institute in Montreal as an out-patient in 1965. I was given three months of talking therapy, which was enough to restore me to productive life, but the main hope to the doctor there was in the new chemical therapies. I was bombarded with countless pills, though the long-term side effects were as yet unknown. Some of these pills really helped and others were actually harmful.

There were ministers who counseled - each finding himself out of his depth. There were the M.D.'s, a psychologist, and a social worker, who varied only in lack of training or inspiration or in ineptness. There were two who I realized were just quacks, voyeurs satisfying their own curiosity and their greed. Most were of good will, and I can't deny that their concern helped me.

I come from a family of activists and, realizing my personal difficulty in finding an adequate mental health provider, I became one of the founders of Carroll County Mental Health in 1965. I knew I couldn't be the only one in need of care. It was through Carroll County Mental Health that I was referred to Dr. Paul D. Lidstrom, who not only listened and cared, but didn't criticize my awkward stumblings or question my beliefs. He did not judge me or bawl me out, no matter how glaring my faults or failures. His respect has given me greater independence and the courage to take risks I wouldn't have dared to take in the past. His encouragement helped me find my voice. I have learned to stand up for my rights, and I am comfortable in my own bones. My faith and trust in the essential goodness of mankind have been vindicated. I have learned new, more appropriate and successful life skills. Anyone can passively listen and care. Paul has been an active listener and teacher. The best teachers gently lead and encourage their students to find the truth in their own ways.

I remembered the intense and therapeutic joy I had found in painting and writing at the Institute of Living, so long ago. To my surprise, Paul liked and encouraged my efforts. **Dreams & Memories** are the art therapy I have created as a patient of Dr. Lidstrom.

I am grateful to my parents, who taught me courage, the love of truth and of hard work carefully executed and finished with attention to detail. They taught me to serve my community, and to be determined and persistent in all my endeavors. I am grateful to my family, my husband, daughters, sister and brother, who have put up with the erratic nature of my behavior and still stuck by me, and to many friends who have given me so much support.

Today, and today is all that counts, as I write this I am miraculously free of depression.

Ask, and it shall be given you; seek, and ye shall find; knock, and it shall be opened unto you…
Or what man is there of you, whom if his son ask for bread, will he give him a stone?

>Matthew: Chapter 7, Verse 7 and 9.

ABOUT THE ARTIST

Born September 7, 1929, in New York City.

I attended public schools in Great Neck, Long Island. After graduating from Northampton School for Girls, in Northampton, Massachusetts, I attended Juilliard School of Music, Barnard College, and the Peabody Music School, between 1948 and 1951. Amy Ellerman and Eloise Deginring were my voice teachers during my college years.

Lawrence H. Sherman and I were married in 1948, and we have two daughters, who are now employed at the University of New Hampshire. Sarah is an associate professor of English and Carrie is a writer and editor in the Communications Department. We have one grandson, Peter Calderwood.

In 1959 we moved to Conway, New Hampshire, to manage Radio Station WBNC. We bought the station in 1960, and in 1968 we started a sister station WMWV, also in Conway.

As a woman in broadcasting, I was a pioneer: one of the first women in sales, management and ownership; first woman on the board of the New Hampshire Association of Broadcasters in 1959 and secretary of that organization for several years; first woman to address the Radio Advertising Bureau, in New York City in 1965.

My duties at the stations were: sales, sales management, promotion, billing and collections. We increased gross sales over eight hundred percent. We started with a staff of five and when we sold the station, in 1989, the staff had increased to fifteen.

I am particularly proud of founding the WMWV Garden Trail, in 1960. This is a gardening contest held throughout the

Mount Washington Valley, open to both amateur and professional gardeners. Prizes are given and the gardens are open to the public. The *Christian Science Monitor* published an article about the program which became syndicated in papers throughout the United States. Another article will appear in *Boston Magazine*. The Garden Trail has made Mount Washington Valley the Garden Spot of New England.

In 1960, I became a council member of Conways' Home Industries, the local affiliate of The League of New Hampshire Craftsmen. I have worked with this group and have served as president for several terms. I was voted a board member of The League of New Hampshire Craftsmen in 1980 and served until 1988. During that time, I was chairman of the nominating committee; served on the search committee for the new executive director and was on the planning, finance, publications, education, and facilities committees. I am proud that I was able to help bring about the new League building in North Conway, by convincing the Conway planning and zoning boards that it was necessary to grandfather the new building. Their vote was unanimous.

I served a second term on the League's foundation board and worked to consolidate and reorganize the League's educational programs. The opportunity was provided by the League for me to take a course in non-profit arts management at Antioch College. In 1991, I accepted the non-paid position as co-chairman for New Hampshire of The Year of American Craft, which took place in 1993. My tin Christmas ornament of a trumpeting angel was displayed on President and Mrs. Clinton's Christmas tree at the White House as part of the celebration of the Year.

I have been on the board of the Mount Washington Valley Arts Association since 1982, serving as president of that organization from 1985 until 1990, and I am now serving as an advisor to this board. I was able to help the nominating committee find a strong working board and to see the Arts Association start a successful gallery for members' work and provide art classes, exhibits, shows, workshops, demonstrations and lectures for the community. I have been nominated twice for the Governor's Award for Patron of the Arts in New Hampshire.

I also served on the board of Arts Jubilee; was a founder and secretary of Carroll County Mental Health; and was the founder and president of Planned Parenthood of Carroll County. Carroll County Mental Health Services director Linda Fox Phillips has asked me to serve on their advisory board for the fall of 1993 and 1994, and I have accepted.

During the years I have lived in New Hampshire, I sang in church choirs, performed in The Resort Players productions and gave a concert for the Conway Women's Club. However, my main focus has been crafts and fine art.

I studied embroidery with Betsy E. Leiper and Susan Rock and have taken many workshops given by The Embroiderers' Guild. I have taken many blue ribbons for my work. I won the Marvis Cohan Award in 1981, and the Southern Maine Chapter of the Embroiderers' Guild's annual award for excellence in embroidery.

I studied rug hooking with Linda Sorensen and Hallie Hall and attended the Green Mountain International Rug Hooking School in Vermont. One of my rugs took the Folk Art Award in the annual juried exhibit of the League of Craftsmen in 1983, and was featured in *Fiber Arts* magazine. My rugs were hung in the Currier Gallery of Art in Manchester, New Hampshire, and in the Des Moines Museum of Art in Des Moines, Iowa.

I teach several crafts: basket making, wearable art, tincraft and Sculpey Clay bead making, for the Embroiderers' Guild, Conways' Home Industries, the Mount Washington Valley Arts Association, Kennett High School, the Madison Library and the Conway Pre-school.

In 1983, I took a "hands on" fine art course with Ellwyn Hayslip from the School of Lifelong Learning. I have studied drawing, watercolor and monoprinting with the Mount Washington Valley Arts Association. Some of these efforts have been on display at The State of the Art Gallery in Jackson, New Hampshire, and are shown periodically at the Mount Washington Valley Arts Association Gallery in North Conway, New Hampshire.

In January of 1991, I was a degree student at the Savannah College of Art and Design, in Savannah, Georgia, where I studied drawing, paper making and basket making. I took a writing workshop with Carolyn Chute, author of *The Beans of Egypt, Maine*, in 1991. During the 1991-92 academic year, I took drawing and painting at the Portland School of Art in Portland, Maine.

In August and September, 1992, **Dreams & Memories** was first shown at the Idia Center in Intervale, New Hampshire. This show, with the addition of new work, was exhibited at The Jumping Off Place in Conway during the summer of 1993. *Family Tree, 1992* is part of the New Hampshire Historical Society's folk art exhibit, "Traditional Roots, Contemporary

Expressions," which runs in Concord, New Hampshire, from February to September 1994.

In November, 1992, my husband and I repurchased WBNC and WMWV. I am sales and promotions manager and supervise the maintenance of the physical plant. In the calendar year of 1993, the stations have shown a thirty percent increase of gross billing. My husband is again the general manager and program director of the stations.

In January of 1991, I registered the name "Heart's Desire" as an art and craft home business. This business markets my work, buys and sells collections of other artists' work, and allows me to act as an art consultant and teacher.

February 22, 1994